Contenders
And
Pretenders

Contenders
And
Pretenders

Who Will Run and Who Will Win the Race for the White House In 2008

Rey Thomas

iUniverse, Inc.
New York Lincoln Shanghai

Contenders And Pretenders
Who Will Run and Who Will Win the Race for the White House In 2008

iUniverse books may be ordered through booksellers or by contacting:

iUniverse
2021 Pine Lake Road, Suite 100
Lincoln, NE 68512
www.iuniverse.com
1-800-Authors (1-800-288-4677)

ISBN-13: 978-0-595-42670-6 (pbk)
ISBN-13: 978-0-595-87000-4 (ebk)
ISBN-10: 0-595-42670-0 (pbk)
ISBN-10: 0-595-87000-7 (ebk)

Printed in the United States of America

For
my family and friends
who have spent hours
listening to me talk
politics.

Contents

Introduction

The race for President of the United States, 2008, is well underway. In American politics, the race is a year-round affair. Because the sitting Vice President, Dick Cheney, has definitively stated he is not going to be a Contender for the nation's highest office, there is no presumptive Republican heir to the Presidency. That leaves a growing number of Contenders, both Democrat and Republican, jockeying to join the battle royal.

Political pundits couldn't ask for more intrigue and neither could the American public. The collective hope is that from these Contenders, voters will hear fresh ideas for the future of our country and the world. Candidates for America's Presidency have a responsibility to convincingly communicate to voters who they are, what they believe and how they plan to deliver on their promises.

One sure fact regarding the past two Democratic Contenders for President was some voters had a difficult time connecting with Al Gore and John Kerry. Ultimately, those voters didn't support candidates that had been so massaged and packaged by political consultants, they were left wondering, "Who are those guys?" Not to say that George W. Bush was not a massaged and packaged candidate. Certainly, he was. But frankly, his guys did a better job of packaging. Comedian Stephen Colbert puts it this way: "George Bush believes on Wednesday what he believed on Monday, no matter what happened on Tuesday."

Fortunately or unfortunately, and events in Iraq and Afghanistan point more towards unfortunately, people buy into that type of blind confidence. They respect it. They vote for it. They did twice. Granted, candidate Bush has changed his tune on the finer points when he became President Bush (i.e., nation building), and the 2006 mid-term election results proved voters had grown uneasy with the direction Bush was leading the country, but that's politics. The first thing you must do is win. Bush won, Gore and Kerry didn't. The question for Gore and Kerry now is whether either can redeem themselves in 2008? The problem for both is they are going to have a great deal of company if they decide to try again.

The issues facing the Contenders for the Presidency are legion: Iraq, immigration, the economy, energy, global warming, the war on terror, Roe v. Wade, The Supreme Court, gay rights and much more. We have already seen the fault lines created within both Parties on the immigration issue; lines that will only grow wider and deeper as election 2008 approaches.

There are twenty-plus men, and women, who have their eyes on the White House. Clinton (Hillary, that is) and McCain being the biggest names among them and the early favorites. No more than ten have a legitimate chance to win. Who are the Contenders? Who are the Pretenders? Who will be the next President of the United States?

Democratic Overview

*"I'm sick and tired of people who say that if you debate and dis-
agree with this administration, somehow you're not patriotic.
We need to stand up and say we're Americans, and we have the
right to debate and disagree with any administration."*
                                                    —Hillary Clinton

When you begin the discussion about who will be the Democratic
nominee for President of the United States, you begin with Hillary
Rodham Clinton. But there are a number of Contenders who will not
only challenge her, but also have the opportunity to defeat her, and
defeat her convincingly.

In 2004, the Democratic Contender possessing the momentum leading into Iowa and New Hampshire was Howard Dean, with the John
Kerry campaign on life support. It's amazing what a couple of weeks and
a few primaries can do. Even with all the money Dean had raised on the
internet, if voters don't think you can win, it will be over in a blink of an
eye. Dean screamed and he was finished. Kerry became the man to beat.

At some point, voters began asking, "Who is Howard Dean and can
he really win?" They loved his fire, his ability to walk the walk and talk
the talk and, most of all, take George Bush to the verbal woodshed, but
they wondered, "Does he truly have the ability to beat Bush in a general
election?" Ultimately, those voters said "Nope" and simultaneously, they
began to believe that Kerry had the stature, the pedigree to win.

One might ask what kind of general election campaign Howard Dean
would have run? He had begun the process of toning down his rhetoric

before Iowa and New Hampshire, the process of "Moving more towards the middle." That is the same process being undertaken by Hillary Clinton. Whether it's Iraq or immigration, the "Middle" is where you need to be, or so that's what many politicians believe.

Hindsight is 20/20 and with hindsight, this question is posed to Democrats: If you knew going in that the Contender you pitted against George Bush would lose in 2004, would you rather have lost with the lackluster campaign of John Kerry or with the fiery campaign of Howard Dean, the Dean before the move to the middle and before "The Scream?"

What kind of campaign will the Democratic Contender run in 2008? Will it be "Hillary, in the middle?" "Kerry, who the hell knows where?" "Obama, new ideas from the new kid on the block?" Below is a list of Democratic Contenders who want to become the next President of the United States:

- Hillary Clinton
- John Kerry
- Al Gore
- John Edwards
- Wesley Clark
- Joe Biden
- Barack Obama
- Tom Vilsack

The Democratic nominee will emerge from these eight Contenders and conventional wisdom says that all eight will run. Yes, that means you too, Al Gore.

All are strong Contenders. Unfortunately, some may prove to be "One trick ponies." A few of those ponies, however, have the potential to cause great harm to the thoroughbreds, which may open the door for a lesser known Contender to emerge (Jimmy Carter, 1976).

In 2000, after eight years as Vice President, Al Gore had his opportunity and lost. In 2004, John Kerry, the Vietnam vet, the safe choice, had his opportunity and lost. In 2008, will Democrats go safe again and will they go home again, sad and defeated? Or will new blood and a new direction emerge?

Republican Overview

"I am a Republican. I'm loyal to the Party of Abraham Lincoln and Theodore Roosevelt. And I believe that my Party, in some ways, has strayed from those principles, particularly on the issue of fiscal discipline."

—John McCain

Beginning in 1804, seven sitting Vice Presidents have attempted to run for President. Only two, George H. W. Bush and Martin Van Buren, were successful. In 2008, Dick Cheney will not be the eighth Vice President to attempt this difficult feat.

That leaves a wide open Republican field, headed by John McCain. In 2000, when Contender Bush was running for the Presidency, he campaigned strategically and successfully on how he would restore "Honor" to the White House; honor that had been sullied by Whitewater, Monica Lewinsky, etc. Al Gore and the Democratic Party were on defense from the get-go.

In 2008, however, after eight years of a Republican Presidency that has seen its share of scandals and questions regarding ethics, it's going to be the GOP Contenders that will have to defend questions about their President's record, not only from Democrats but from within their own Party as well. Iraq, immigration, fiscal discipline are just some of the issues that threaten to violently shake the core of the GOP.

John McCain, in 2004 at the Republican National Convention, said that the mission in Iraq was "Necessary, achievable and noble." He, or whoever is the Republican nominee, must defend that statement to a public that grows more skeptical of the war day after day. Ironically, there will be many Democrats that will have to defend their own statements on the war; defend their decision, as Senators, to vote in the affirmative for the Iraq War Resolution in 2002.

Which Republican Contender will be able to hold onto the GOP base, including Christian Conservatives, while at the same time making the Party more attractive to Moderates who are uneasy about the Iraq war, immigration and the economy? Below is a list of Republicans who will throw their hat in the ring to become the next President of the United States:

- John McCain
- Rudy Guliani
- Sam Brownback
- Mike Huckabee
- Mitt Romney
- Newt Gingrich
- Chuck Hagel
- George Pataki

The Republican nominee will emerge from these eight Contenders. Like the Democrats, the heavy-hitters might run into some tough competition from lesser known Contenders and just as it was in 1960 with JFK, religious affiliation will be a major factor in the selection process.

Can John McCain make a lasting peace with Christian Conservatives? Can Rudy Guliani overcome his Pro-Choice stance? How will Mitt Romney's Mormon faith play in the South? Who will be left standing?

Red State, Blue State

"Election by election, state by state, precinct by precinct, door by door, vote by vote, we're going to lift our Party up and take this country back for the people who built it."
—Howard Dean

In the 2000 Presidential election, Al Gore did not win a Southern state below Maryland. In 2004, John Kerry did not win a Southern state below Maryland. It took two consecutive defeats but finally somebody in the Democratic Party realized that in order for Democrats to become viable nationally again, they'll need a national strategy. While future success for Democrats may not start in Dixie, their bad habit of writing off large swaths of territory must come to an end.

In February, 2005, when Howard Dean was elected chairman of the Democratic National Committee, many in his Party thought he would do to the Committee what he did to his Presidential campaign: Crash it and burn.

Dean, without question, is a lightning rod who sometimes says things better left unsaid but no one can argue that before his campaign disintegrated, he infused the Democratic Party with an energy that had been lacking for a number of years.

Unlike the eventual nominee, John Kerry, Dean was able to cogently attack President Bush in particular and the Republican Party in general about the war in Iraq. What he was not able to do was convince voters in Iowa and New Hampshire that he was the best candidate to challenge

Bush in November, 2004. However, his most important work for his Party may well lie in the years ahead.

For far too long, Democrats have written off Southern, Midwest and Mountain states in Presidential elections and in doing so have basically written off the state and local Party organizations. Before election night begins, Democrats know they will be one hundred and fifty electoral votes in the hole.

2000 and 2004 were clear examples of a national political strategy that needed to be revised. It's embarrassing enough that Gore and Kerry won no Southern states below Maryland. It's worse when a sitting Vice President can't win his home state of Tennessee as well as his President's home state of Arkansas. You want to write off the South, go ahead but you've got to find a way to win at least ONE of those two states. If Gore had, Florida would have been meaningless.

Historically, the South started moving away from Democrats in the late 50's and early 60's. Civil rights, the war in Vietnam, the rise of the Dixiecrats and other factors contributed to the growing tide of conservative Republicans below the Mason-Dixon Line.

There were exceptions in national elections: Lyndon Johnson defeating a demagogue Barry Goldwater; Jimmy Carter defeating a Watergate-ridden Gerald Ford; and Bill Clinton defeating an out-of-touch George H.W. Bush and a sacrificial lamb Bob Dole.

Aside from those elections, the South remained a Republican stronghold, specifically at the state and local level. What Howard Dean has realized is that for Democrats to regain large blocs of the country that have moved towards the political Right, they must invest time and money in those areas. Hence, Dean's "50-State Strategy."

Although Rahm Emanuel, chairman of the Democratic Congressional Campaign Committee and his counterpart in the Senate, Chuck Schumer, may have been at odds with Dean prior to the mid-term elections in 2006 regarding which races the DNC should infuse money into, Democratic victories in that year proved inside and outside the Democratic Party that Dean's strategy had merit. James Carville may still remain a doubter but his calls for Dean's ouster after the mid-terms went largely unheeded.

Much like the success businesses in Japan gleaned for many years by looking at company performance, not a year or two forward but a decade or two forward, Dean's strategy demonstrated to Democratic operatives that they must decide what constitutes victory more than one election cycle at a time. Many in the Party felt additional campaign money should have been funneled to fewer Congressional races in 2006, whereas Dean wanted Democratic candidates to be competitive in places like Idaho, Utah, Kansas, Mississippi, Montana and Wyoming; places where Washington beltway moneymen and consultants, like Carville, believed were a waste of time.

But state Democratic Party leaders have praised Dean for helping them get back in the game again. In many districts where Republican incumbents were thought to be safe, the GOP had to play defense and spend money to hold onto their seats. To the surprise of some Republicans nationwide, they lost control of both the House and the Senate.

Republicans now have to revisit their national strategy in the years to come because of the gains made by Democrats. After the 2006 mid-terms, Republicans still have a strong hold on the South, but they have lost ground everywhere else. It's clear that the war in Iraq has been a drag on the fortunes of the GOP. Although many leading Democrats will be on the defensive regarding their initial support for the invasion of Iraq, Republicans will get the worse of a public's sour mood as the war grows deadlier since "Mission Accomplished" was proclaimed.

Also, many Reagan Conservatives and Christian Conservatives are disillusioned with the direction that President Bush and Neo-

Conservatives have taken the GOP. While the battle for the heart and soul of the Republican Party rages, Independents, who make up a majority of the voting public and who had been a reliable part of the Republican majority, are starting to move closer to the Democrats. Those Independents provided the winning margins for Democrats in the 2006 mid-term elections.

Swing states like Ohio, now with a Democrat in the Governor's mansion, and Missouri are turning bluer. Red states like Arizona and Colorado are starting to bleed red and turn purple. Iraq, uncontrolled government spending, scandals, immigration and an overall sense the country is headed in the wrong direction are issues that must be intelligently addressed by the Republican Party and their next Presidential nominee in order to stop the electoral map hemorrhaging.

For most, George Bush the candidate in 2000 possessed attributes acceptable to the many factions of the GOP. Since he has been a disappointment to some in those factions, it will be much more difficult for the next Republican nominee to gain consensus support. More importantly, that nominee will have to bring back Independents and Moderates which may mean taking positions not agreeable to Christian Conservatives or Neo-Conservatives. It will require a balancing act.

It's a balancing act that might be easier for a Republican and harder for a Democrat. A Republican nominee who positions himself as a Reagan Conservative would have a very good chance of regaining those Republican, Independent and Moderate voters that have turned away from George Bush. Those red states may be bleeding, but they are far from bled out.

A Democratic nominee MUST find a way to break through in red states. Pinning hopes for electoral success on Ohio and Florida alone will not work for Democrats; ask Gore and Kerry. Also, Howard Dean's 50-State Strategy, while it aided state and local candidates in 2006, may take more than one election cycle to help a Presidential Contender. A Democratic nominee needs to be able through his, or her, own identity convince moderate-to-conservative Democrats and Independents in red states that they have 50-state appeal.

Who in the Democratic Party with visions of the Presidency can accomplish this feat? Gore and Kerry have both proven they were not equal to the task. Can either of them, eight and four years removed respectively, change their past outcomes in 2008? Do Democratic voters even want to give them the opportunity?

Hillary Clinton might be the 2008 version of Gore and Kerry. Looking at the electoral map, it's hard to see what red states her candidacy would put in play. Most polling data also shows her with some of the highest negative ratings of all the major Contenders, both Democrat and Republican. She is a well-known commodity and this election may be shaping up to be an opportunity for an unknown commodity to break out of the pack.

Hillary also carries the baggage of having voted in favor of the Iraq war Resolution in 2002. John Kerry, John Edwards and Joe Biden join her as Democratic Senators having to worry about that vote as well. That issue alone may be enough to greatly damage all of them early in the primaries which might open the door for a lesser known entity to enter.

Democrats need a Contender with more national appeal. Republicans need a Contender who is less polarizing than the current Republican President. Both Parties are acutely aware and the 2006 midterm elections confirmed that red state-blue state America is changing significantly. What worked in the past two decades may not work in 2008, which means that the names of Contenders at the top of most lists may not be the eventual nominee for either Party.

Kerry & Gore, Part II?

"I haven't made a Sherman statement, but that's not an effort to hold the door open. It's more the internal shifting of gears. I can't imagine any circumstances in which I would become a candidate again. I've found other ways to serve. I'm enjoying them."

—Al Gore

"I will be voting to give the President of the United States the authority to use force if necessary to disarm Saddam Hussein because I believe that a deadly arsenal of weapons of mass destruction in his hands is a real and grave threat to our security."

—John Kerry

In 1962, two years after losing the Presidency by the slimmest of margins to John F. Kennedy, Richard Nixon lost the California Governor's race to Pat Brown. In his concession speech, Nixon told the gathered media this was going to be his last press conference and he spoke words that had a Civil War General William Sherman-like quality to them: "You don't have Dick Nixon to kick around anymore."

Well, it was just a matter of time before the press and public did have Dick Nixon to kick around some more because the pull of the national political stage was too much for Nixon to resist. After moving to New York and making a great deal of money as a senior partner in a law firm bearing his name, Nixon spent 1966 traveling the country campaigning for Republican candidates running in Congressional elections, much like Gore did in 2006. He rebuilt his base of support within the

Republican Party. He became the Contender that could reclaim the White House for the GOP.

Which begs the question: Will Al Gore in 2008 be what Nixon became after his first failed attempt at the White House? Will Gore, like Nixon, have the moment when those in his Party turn their eyes toward him and say, "Hey, you know what: He lost his last time out but right now, he looks like our best shot. He can get it back for us. He's our guy. He's the one for now."

Gore is going to need much more than a campaign against global warming for Democratic voters to forget about the election of 2000 and give him another shot and he just might have it in the Iraq war. Since the buildup leading to the war, Gore has consistently been a vocal critic of the Bush administration's planning, or lack thereof and execution. Gore did, however, support George H.W. Bush and the Persian Gulf War. Many voters, regardless of Party affiliation, would say Gore was right in both cases. This would put him at odds with John Kerry who initially supported the current war in Iraq, before changing his mind. Kerry, by the way, voted against the Resolution in 1991 regarding the Persian Gulf War.

Any Democratic Senator that voted "Yea" on Resolution 114 in 2002 need only remind themselves of the difficulty John Kerry had during his entire campaign against George Bush trying to explain that vote. He never has coherently done so to this day. Who's to say that any of those Senators, Hillary included, will do any better in 2008? And Kerry's statement, "I actually did vote for the $87 billion before I voted against it," regarding the supplemental funding bill for U.S. troops in Iraq and Afghanistan, may forever keep him to just visitor status on his trips to the White House.

Kerry and Gore face two fundamental questions: Will either one have the desire necessary to make another run for the Presidency and do Democratic voters want to give them another opportunity?

In Gore's case, it's obvious the decision whether to run again is going to be significantly harder. He has been out of the game longer and his loss in 2000 left much deeper wounds than Kerry's loss did him. Gore won the popular vote against Bush and lost by four electoral votes. Kerry lost by three percentage points in the popular vote and 34 electoral votes.

Frankly, one could look at Gore and see a man who is more comfortable with himself than at any time in his political life. He's relaxed, he has a cause to pursue that he truly believes is worth the fight and the pressures of politics seem worlds away. His waistline alone is proof that filet mignon, lobster, caviar and champagne in Cannes are much more pleasing to the body and soul than rubber chicken on the campaign trail. Still, many sense it's just a matter of time before Gore throws his hat in the ring, possibly the only person that can stop the "Hillary Train."

But how will the public react? More importantly, how will the Democratic primary voters respond? After the 2000 election was over and the post mortems began, many Democrats were upset with the campaign Al Gore ran. Most thought Bush was a lightweight and a sitting Vice President, who was sailing with the winds of a growing economy, federal budget surplus and relative world peace blowing through his campaign sails, should coast to victory. But an impeached President still occupying the Oval Office can certainly ruin a Contender's day.

"We could squander this moment but our country would be the poorer for it. Instead, let's lift our eyes and see how wide the American horizon has become. We're entering a new time. We're electing a new President. And I stand here tonight as my own man."

When Al Gore spoke these words in his acceptance speech at the Democratic National Convention in Los Angeles in 2000, many rightly assumed this was his way of attempting to separate himself from the transgressions of his boss, President Bill Clinton. In 1998, Clinton became the second President to be impeached by the House of Representatives. The Monica Lewinsky scandal certainly caused a foul odor to hang over the final two years of the Clinton administration.

In addition, Gore's selection of Connecticut Senator Joe Lieberman as his running mate sought to further insulate the Democratic ticket from the Clinton scandal. Lieberman was a fierce critic of Clinton's actions and was portrayed as a highly religious man who would help Gore bring honor back to the White House. Interestingly, it was George Bush, who's campaign on bringing honor back to the White House, that was more effective; more than Gore's attempt to stand on his own or his selection of Lieberman.

But why would Gore decide to run from Clinton? Although people may have been weary of the soap opera that the Clinton administration had become, Clinton himself was still popular, America was in a strong economic position and the majority of the public felt positively about the country's present and future.

Many voters also had a difficult time waiting for the "Real Al Gore" to stand up. Much of his primary and general election campaign was spent trying to personally define who he was and what his positions were. Some of this can be attributed to a mainstream and secondary media which didn't shy away from portraying Gore as wooden and boring. His average to poor performances in the debates didn't help either, especially coupled with Bush's passing performances on what were very low expectations.

Ultimately, George Bush and Karl Rove ran a better campaign than Al Gore and Donna Brazile. Gore never found his footing and Bush stayed on message, ad nauseam maybe but conclusively to victory. Gore's decision to go it alone, to keep Clinton tucked away in the White House contributed to his defeat. Only in the last few days of the election did Clinton get out on the campaign trail when Gore's campaign knew things might be slipping away from them but it was already too late. An election finally was lost on five hundred and thirty seven votes in Florida.

What would be different for Gore this time around? His campaign in 2000 was much closer to the Left of the political spectrum than were the eight previous years he had spent in the Clinton administration. Even his former running mate, Lieberman, was critical of Gore for running too strongly on the populist theme of "People versus the powerful."

His embrace of the global warming issue, most notably portrayed in the book and movie "An Inconvenient Truth," has made him a darling of the Left but won't necessarily make him any more attractive to the people who didn't vote for him the first time around. For Gore, does it come down again to Ohio and Florida? Can Democrats take that chance once more with him?

The issue for Gore, which most likely will be the defining issue for all the Contenders, will be Iraq. If it continues to be a military quagmire, those, like Gore, who opposed it, will get traction. But how much? While opposition to the war in Iraq is now shared by the majority of Americans, what is the solution? Will the American public be subjected to another election season of, "stay the course," "cut and run," "timetables" and "benchmarks," dominating the election discussion?

No question, this is a different Al Gore from the one last seen in 2000. He's looser, he's speaking his mind. He's the guy everybody wanted to see years ago. But will that translate into votes? Does his electoral map remain the same shade of red and blue?

As difficult as it might be for Al Gore to decide whether he has a chance to win in 2008, it probably is downright impossible for John Kerry not to want to redeem himself after his debacle in 2004. Kerry has already made it clear he's most likely going to be a Contender in 2008. He's got a pretty hefty war chest left from his campaign and he still feels he was sullied and misrepresented by Bush, Rove and the Swift Boat controversy.

If Bill Clinton was "The Comeback Kid," John Kerry could have been called "Lazarus," because he definitely rose from the political dead in the 2004 Democratic primaries. Coming into Iowa and New Hampshire, Kerry was running out of money and looked to have no shot at the nomination. Howard Dean was a juggernaut that looked unstoppable. All the polls had Dean with a comfortable lead, he had plenty of cash on hand and he had the endorsement of the previous Democratic nominee, Al Gore.

Kerry seemed to be dead on arrival but eventually the voters in the first two states to cast ballots felt Kerry had a better chance to unseat George Bush and their feelings were shown by large margins. In the Iowa caucuses, Kerry received 38%, John Edwards 32% and Dean 18%. Days later in the New Hampshire primary, Kerry garnered 39% of the vote while Dean came in second with 26%. For Dean, the money began to dry up, while for Kerry, he rode the resurgence to the nomination.

Kerry chose John Edwards as his running mate knowing that Edwards was a fresh, young face in the Party and a Southerner. On paper, it looked to be a potent combination. Kerry also decided to deflect any questions about whether he would be strong on defense by highlighting his Vietnam war service, going so far as to announce at the beginning of his acceptance speech at the Democratic National Convention in Boston that "I'm John Kerry and I'm reporting for duty" as he saluted the audience.

It's still amazing to remember that a man who actually volunteered to serve in Vietnam would allow himself to be portrayed as weak, soft on defense and unable to protect the American people but that is exactly what happened to John Kerry. The country was just beginning to realize that Iraq was going to be a long hard slog and the three men who were the face of that war, President Bush, Vice President Dick Cheney and Secretary of Defense Donald Rumsfeld, had never served a day in Vietnam. But once the Swift Boat Ads began to play around the country, the American public began to develop serious questions about Kerry's Vietnam service and his fitness to be President.

Even worse for Kerry, the controversy over the ads by the "Swift Boat Veterans for Truth" began during the weeks between political conventions, when both Parties normally refrain from partisan attacks. While attempting to take the political high road by quietly denouncing the ad, Kerry and his campaign unbelievably failed to recognize the damage it was doing to his image. Here was a man running for President, who had received five medals for his service in Vietnam, who would now have that service in wartime portrayed negatively.

Kerry never fought back strongly and it made him look weak. Bush's campaign brilliantly had the President himself criticize the ad, making it an issue about the 527's and soft campaign money being bad for the political system and all the while insulating him from any connection to the Swift Boat Veterans. Kerry needed to forget about the high road, forget about the tradition of no partisan politics between conventions and forget about the fact that the Swift Boat Veterans had no "Official" connection to the Bush campaign.

Kerry's strength was being questioned and he had no answer. He needed to address the Swift Boat controversy from the moment it began and he should have attacked Bush, Cheney and Rumfeld's lack of military service to his outrage. He should have said, "How dare those that never served question my fitness to defend my country? How dare a President who stayed stateside to help with his daddy's political campaign question me, a soldier who volunteered to defend his country, about whether or not I'm strong on defense? I defended my country. Where were you? I served in Vietnam. Where were you? Where was Cheney? Where was Rumsfeld? How dare you men who never served in wartime send other men off to war without any real idea of what you're getting our country into or how to get us out? How dare you? I say that you, Mr. President, and those that serve for you are unfit to defend our great country, and as President, I will finish this war that you so cavalierly started and I will finish it with victory. I will bring our men and women home safely and never again will I allow those that never tasted battle in their lives to put our country at risk."

That's what he should have said. Instead, he went windsurfing. One wonders if Kerry ever saw the classic Vietnam War movie, "Apocalypse Now," and heard the famous line spoken by Robert Duvall's character: "Charlie don't surf!" Well, neither should a Contender for President of the United States when he's getting pummeled by people calling him weak. Kerry's inability or lack of desire to respond forcefully played right into his critic's hands.

It wasn't until Kerry made a slip of the tongue while campaigning in California just before the mid-term elections in 2006 did he decide to fight his critics but once again, he was put on the defensive and made to look, if not stupid, ignorant of the statements that come out of his mouth. While trying to make a joke about President Bush, his words were turned against him by Republicans to make it seem he insulted the troops in Iraq. Along with high-profile Republicans, even Democrats, like Harold Ford, who was locked in a tough race for Senate in Tennessee which he eventually lost, asked Kerry to apologize. As Yogi Berra once said, it was déjà vu all over again.

Nothing Kerry said or did leading up to Election Day 2004 changed enough minds about whether he was too weak to lead. He didn't distinguish himself at all from Bush in the debates and his campaign had an unbelievable air of supreme confidence that he was going to win the election. In Kerry's mind, he was sure the voters "Got it." They had to know that he was smarter, better prepared, more qualified to serve than George Bush. What Kerry failed to realize is voters just didn't "Get him." They also had a difficult time not seeing him as a flip-flopper, changing his mind on the war in Iraq and the 2002 Senate Resolution, amongst other things.

Kerry now says that if he does decide to run in 2008, he will not allow himself to be "Swift-Boated" like he was in 2004. Unfortunately, that statement of strength may be four years too late for Democratic voters to give him another chance to win their respect or the Democratic nomination. As far as those voters are concerned, Gore lost to Bush but Kerry let himself get beaten by a vulnerable Commander In Chief. The former may be more forgivable than the latter.

It's All About Hillary and McCain

"Our political differences, no matter how sharply they are debated, are really quite narrow in comparison to the remarkably durable national consensus on our founding convictions."
—John McCain

John McCain spoke words that many Americans wish were true. Not since the 60's have people in this country been so polarized along Party lines. War has a way of doing that and Iraq has not disappointed in making those divisions deep.

Obviously, the names of Presidential Contenders most discussed are Hillary Clinton and John McCain. McCain has been down this road before, losing a brutal and sometimes ugly primary battle against the current President. But Hillary, after winning a landslide re-election in the New York Senate race, will be a Presidential race neophyte. Does she really have a chance?

Since the age of sixteen when she campaigned for Barry Goldwater in 1964, Hillary Clinton has been involved in politics and her marriage to Bill Clinton formed a partnership of politicos that not only wanted to genuinely lead but also yearned for the power that came with winning in the political arena.

From her time as Arkansas's First Lady through her eight years as First Lady of the United States, Hillary Clinton has been an integral part of the success her husband attained as America's 42nd president. Many attribute her "Standing by my man" appearance on 60 Minutes, where she and her husband faced down charges of his infidelity, with helping to save his campaign and catapult him into the White House.

Now it's Bill's turn to stand by his woman. Since her first victory, Bill Clinton has remained supportive of his wife and she has gone from junior Senator to presumptive Democratic nominee for President in 2008. But ultimately, he may be the one person to tell her what some outside and inside the Democratic Party sense to be true: Hillary Clinton may win the Democratic nomination for President but it is impossible for her to win the general election.

While she may lead in early polls, she also has the highest negative ratings of the top Democratic Contenders. She has been since 1993 and remains to this day a highly polarizing figure and Republican strategists have moved from pounding the former President Clinton to criticizing their new bogeywoman, Senator Clinton.

Those Republican strategists would jump for joy if Hillary is the Democratic nominee in 2008 because they know she would be afflicted with the same malady that cursed Gore and Kerry in their runs for the Presidency: The inability to change the red state-blue state electoral map. Where and how does a polarizing figure like Senator Hillary Clinton break through the Republican stranglehold on the South? What Midwest and Mountain states does she swing her way? What else can she put in play, especially if she's matched against John McCain? Is it going to come down to Ohio and Florida again?

Democratic voters need to be significantly more discerning in choosing their 2008 Presidential nominee after seeing two candidates enter 2000 and 2004 with such high hopes only to be defeated in mirror images: Laying too much hope on too few states. Hillary Clinton would also start her run for the White House with higher negative ratings than either Gore or Kerry and that's before the Republican campaign machine figures out how to Swift-Boat her.

After two heartbreaking defeats, Democratic voters may ultimately decide that Hillary is not worth the chance. Winning the nomination is a long way from defeating a Republican candidate, whoever he is, that won't have the incredible onslaught of negative campaigning that will be hurled at Hillary Clinton.

From a financial standpoint, Hillary has a solid amount of cash-on-hand going into 2008, although she spent a great deal of capital on a Senate re-election whose outcome was never in doubt. She also has the ability to raise more cash quickly should she formally announce, probably faster than any other Democratic Contender.

But as Howard Dean learned in 2004, large amounts of campaign financing are not a predictor of future success. The same fate easily could befall Hillary and the question she, her advisors and her husband must ask themselves is simple: Can she really win?

It is possible for Hillary Clinton to be more important to the Democratic Party as a strong leader in the Senate, a Democratic Senate with high profile committee Chairmanships in the balance or as an integral Cabinet level appointee in a Democratic Presidency, just not hers. How much more difficult would that be from an ego perspective if she turns out to be the ex-Presidential candidate that was embarrassed in the primaries?

The allure of the Presidency may eventually be too strong for her to resist but she may find out from the voters that there are other Democratic Contenders with a better opportunity to regain the White House. If she is lucky, someone in her circle of advisors will get that message to her before the voters do.

John McCain is in a much better position nationally in comparison to Hillary Clinton but he is sure to run into strong resistance in the unlikeliest of places: His own Party. McCain has been running for

President since he lost in 2000 and along with Rudy Giuliani, he finds himself at the top of most early polls.

McCain came close in 2000. He skipped the Iowa caucuses and instead focused his attention on the New Hampshire primary. He was not disappointed. He won big in New Hampshire and then set his sights on South Carolina.

But a closer look inside the New Hampshire numbers showed that while McCain won a state with an open primary and a large Independent electorate, the eventual nominee, George Bush, won a significantly larger percentage of voters that identified themselves as Conservatives.

This may be a problem that McCain will face in 2008 as well. He is well-known to be a man with a fierce independent streak which is something that attracts him to moderate Republicans and Democrats but also can make him less attractive to the Republican base, including the Religious Right and the Neo-Conservatives who maintain positions of power within the Republican Party.

McCain proceeded to lose the South Carolina primary. The Bush campaign, with help from Pat Robertson and Jerry Falwell, turned out that state's evangelical voters which greatly tipped the balance in Bush's favor. McCain was never able to recover. He only won four of thirteen states on Super Tuesday and Bush was able to permanently close the door with additional wins in California and New York.

Will McCain be able to beat back a challenger who is perceived to be more conservative, more agreeable to the Religious Right than he? That certainly won't be Giuliani, but what about Romney, Gingrich, Allen, Brownback or Huckabee? As with Hillary Clinton, the most dangerous position for any frontrunner will be the early primaries. There is a great deal of expectation weighing down McCain and any early stumble would present a great opportunity for a dark horse candidate to emerge.

There is a battle going on within the Republican Party, and there is no consensus on whether the Reagan Conservatives and/or the Religious Right will be able to wrest control from the Neo-Conservatives. Those Neo-Cons may be dying but they're not dead yet. All the wings of the GOP will have Contenders running that would be considered acceptable from a policy perspective, so there is no guarantee that McCain goes into Iowa or New Hampshire with any more steam than the other Contenders and a very large field will make it even more difficult.

If Iraq is still the quagmire it has become, voters may be looking for a Contender with strong military credentials to come forward with a plan for victory that has so far evaded the current administration. McCain is a certified war hero. Although that didn't help him win the nomination in 2000 and John Kerry's war service didn't help him win the general election in 2004, the American public might be much more interested in voting for a Contender with previous military experience, especially with 150,000 troops in Iraq.

McCain's plan is to put more troops on the ground in Iraq. He has been highly critical of the Bush administration for not sending enough troops to properly secure Iraq initially, but will Americans, in 2009 in a McCain administration, be willing to put more of their men and women in harm's way? March, 2008, will mark five years with American troops in Iraq. McCain would be inheriting a pessimistic public and a stretched military, both potentially at their breaking points.

If he made it to the general election, McCain would be a formidable foe for any Democratic challenger. Other than Wesley Clark's military service, no potential Democratic Contender can match McCain's credentials, and Clark is far from having what it takes to secure the Democratic nomination. But for McCain, getting to the general election just might be even harder this time around.

Can A Senator Win?

"I don't think any Senator can win the nomination. If they get the nomination, they won't be elected president. I don't think Senators make good candidates, actually, because of what we do. If you're in the Senate for 10 or 15 years, there's a good chance you've voted on both sides of every issue."

—Trent Lott

Trent Lott must have been thinking of Senator John Kerry when he spoke those words. The campaign that Karl Rove ran against Kerry spent as much time telling the public about Kerry's supposed multiple positions on issues as it did espousing the success of the first four years of the George Bush administration.

Kerry didn't help himself either. The infamous "I voted for the 87 billion dollars before I voted against it" was played in attack ad form relentlessly and it definitely portrayed Kerry as a potential Flip-Flopper in Chief. The public doesn't zero in on the day-to-day voting process in the Senate and as Trent Lott said, Senators can and do find themselves casting a yea vote one hour and a nay vote the next, all due to multiple changes that occur to a piece of legislation. If you're John Kerry, that may have been the case, but trying to explain your way out of it can be difficult or for him, impossible.

It's been forty seven years since a sitting Senator was elected to the presidency; his name was John F. Kennedy. The last sitting member of the House of Representatives to achieve that feat was James Garfield in 1880. No wonder Dick Gephardt finally gave up trying.

Other than seeking the Presidency as a sitting Vice President, the most common way of getting to the Oval Office has been through the Governor's mansion and most recently, four out of the last five Presidents elected to office served as Governors. Both Bill Clinton and George W. Bush were sitting Governors while Jimmy Carter was one year removed and Ronald Reagan five years removed from their Governorships.

Why Governors? Many say that as the top state executive it's easier for a Governor to step into the top federal executive seat and be successful; balancing budgets, working with the opposition Party, finding common ground on legislation, etc. They also, as Trent Lott said, don't bring a voting record to the campaign that Senators do, sitting or otherwise, which can be used against them effectively. They are generally, on a national basis, a clean slate.

What they also don't bring to the table is any foreign policy experience and it seems that now in a post 9/11 world, with a war raging in Iraq and potential hotspots in Iran, North Korea and Lebanon, lack of foreign policy experience may make it more difficult for an untested Governor to gain the public's confidence. As the war in Iraq becomes what will greatly define the success or failure of the George Bush administration, will America be ready to again trust a Governor unproven in foreign policy with her future?

The previous two Presidential administrations have also created an atmosphere of toxic political divisiveness that has clearly taken a toll on the American public. There is a growing chorus of voters who yearn for an administration that governs not from the Left or Right but from the Middle. Issues like Iraq, abortion, stem cell research and gay marriage have been and will continue to be battlegrounds until the next administration is sworn in and well after.

There then presents an opportunity for a Contender who is well-known, not less-known, to find success in 2008. Whereas in years past voters have yearned for a fresh face with new ideas and been rewarded, or saddled, with Bill Clinton and George Bush, those voters now want some concrete answers for domestic and international issues and it may be a proven and known commodity, like a Senator, that might fit the bill.

The lineup of Senators on both sides of the aisle is loaded with men and women who come with long years of service and who are well known to the populace. John McCain has served twenty years in the Senate; Joe Biden thirty-four years; Chuck Hagel ten years; Chris Dodd twenty-six years. When the election rolls around in 2008, Hillary Clinton will have eight years in the Senate under her belt.

Lack of experience will also be an issue voters will be looking at closely and there are two names on the Democratic side that are receiving a great deal of interest that may not have the experience to pass muster: John Edwards and Barack Obama. Edwards completed one six year term in the Senate before giving up his seat to run as John Kerry's Vice President in 2004. Obama began serving in the Senate in 2005. He will have between two and three years experience in the Senate before he decides to mount a bid for the Presidency, should he make that decision. Both men are two relatively fresh faces that just may not have enough experience to satisfy what will surely be an overly critical electorate.

Unless there are significant events that change the situation on the ground, Iraq, and what the United States hopes to achieve there, will continue to remain the number one issue on the minds of voters leading up to the 2008 elections. A Commander In Chief with some foreign policy experience may prove to be a pre-requisite which voters find mandatory.

Top-Tier Democratic Contenders

"It took a lot of blood, sweat and tears to get to where we are today, but we have just begun. Today we begin in earnest the work of making sure that the world we leave our children is just a little bit better than the one we inhabit today."

—Barack Obama

It hasn't taken Barack Obama long to become a major player in the Democratic Party. Many attribute part of the success Democrats garnered in the 2006 mid-term elections to the popularity of the first-term Senator from Illinois. Other than former President Bill Clinton, no Democrat was more in demand on the campaign trail than Obama.

Everywhere he campaigned, crowds were huge and enthusiastic. But can he transfer enthusiasm from 2006 to 2008 in a run for the Presidency? That is a question all of the potential Contenders, and their lurking financial donors, are beginning to ask about Obama and everyone else.

Let's take a quick look at the top-tier Democrats who are thinking of jumping into the race for President. As we do, we're going to ask six specific questions:

1. *Who* are they?
2. *What* makes them a Contender?
3. *Where* are they in the public's consciousness?
4. *When/Will* they declare their candidacy?

5. *Why* do they think they can win?

6. *How* can they win?

How these questions are answered will determine whether these Contenders have legitimate chances of being elected or if they are positioning themselves for the number two spot on the ticket or a plum position in a Presidential Cabinet.

Hillary Clinton
Who

It's impossible not to know Hillary Clinton. She is the junior Senator from New York, recently re-elected to a second six-year term in a landslide victory. She is the wife of one of the most popular, yet polarizing Presidents of our time and she herself is a figure that causes many on the far Right of the political spectrum to foam at the mouth.

What

She is the Democratic Contender with the highest name recognition and she will have the largest financial war chest should she decide to declare her candidacy. If she wins in Iowa and New Hampshire, the race for the Democratic nomination would be over.

Where

The public views Hillary Clinton with caution. Many Republicans and Conservatives dislike her but respect her chances to be a formidable opponent in 2008. They do not underestimate her political abilities. Within the Democratic Party, most view her service as a Senator very highly but there is also a large contingent of Democrats who don't believe she can win a general election and sense her nomination could be a disaster. In opinion polls, her negative ratings sometimes match or exceed her positives.

When/Will

Unlike many lesser-known Contenders, she does not need to announce her candidacy early, although Barack Obama's popularity might cause her to do so. With money in the bank, she can wait to announce and still not lose ground. There isn't much doubt she will decide to run.

Why

Other than Obama, no other Democrat brings what Hillary brings to the game: Name recognition, money and power. But with Democrats in control of Congress, there may be other opportunities for her to be a major powerbroker. Might that be enough to persuade her to skip a Presidential campaign that has a huge potential to go horribly wrong?

How

Hillary will have to beat back some fierce competition to win the Democratic nomination and that will not be easy. If she does declare, she can't afford to stumble in Iowa or New Hampshire, although she may decide to skip Iowa. That would mean winning those contests by comfortable margins. If a John Edwards or Barack Obama has a strong showing early, they could become the anti-Hillary candidate and gather enough momentum to destroy any chance she has and if Al Gore decides to jump into the race, all bets are truly off the table. She could turn into Howard Dean, version 2008: Tons of money at the start and gone in a blink of the eye. A general election victory could be even more difficult.

John Kerry
Who

The standard bearer for the Democratic Party in 2004, John Kerry is the junior Senator from Massachusetts. After his defeat by George Bush, Kerry has maintained a high profile in the public eye while contemplating what is sure to be another attempt at the White House in 2008.

What

Kerry still has high name recognition and like Hillary Clinton, a significant war chest remaining from the 2004 campaign. He would be able to tap into a large network of supporters nationwide if he decided to run again and many of those supporters feel he was unjustly Swift-Boated by George Bush and itch for a chance at redemption.

Where

Since the end of the 2004 campaign, Kerry has had difficulty convincing the public that he is not either a flip-flopper or weak on defense. His attempted joke, directed at George Bush that went wrong during the 2006 mid-term elections, was yet another example he has difficulty communicating effectively.

When/Will

Kerry would need to declare very early in order to beat down the naysayers who feel he has no chance of winning the Democratic nomination. It will be necessary for him to completely rebuild his image from the ground up and not very many observers think that is at all possible.

Why

Like his supporters, Kerry believes in 2004 he allowed the Bush campaign to define him, especially with the Swift Boat controversy. He has said should he decide to run again, he will fight back earlier and stronger against attempts to portray him negatively. Unfortunately, this newly discovered bravado might be too little, too late.

How

Kerry can't win the Presidency, let alone the Democratic nomination. He shouldn't enter the race. The joke gone wrong was another example that his skills as a politician are weak. He is prone to say things that the opposition will twist and he will always be on the defensive against any Republican candidate.

Al Gore
Who

The standard bearer for the Democratic Party in 2000, the former Vice President took a much needed sabbatical after his gut-wrenching loss to George Bush. Although he won the popular vote, Gore lost the election after coming up five hundred and thirty seven votes short in Florida. That state's twenty five electoral votes, and the Presidency, were awarded to Bush.

What

Unlike John Kerry, Al Gore has convincingly rehabilitated his image since losing in 2000. Many in the Democratic Party see him as the only Contender that could beat back a Hillary Clinton candidacy should she decide to run.

Where

Gore's book and movie, "An Inconvenient Truth," were widely praised and made him the point man of the movement to fight global warming, which will be a major issue in 2008. The public sees a person much more comfortable and at ease with himself in Gore, unlike the candidate they saw in 2000.

When/Will

Like Hillary Clinton, Gore can wait to announce his candidacy at the last possible moment should he choose. Money and support would flow his way relatively quickly and he may be taking a wait and see attitude as it pertains to Clinton. If she enters, many may pressure him to do the same.

Why

While he has come to terms with his defeat in 2000, Gore still believes he is destined for the Presidency. He knows he's not the only candidate to fail on his first attempt only to succeed the next time around and eight years may have been just enough time for him to get the competitive juices flowing again.

How

Gore has been to this dance before and unlike John Kerry, Democrats could see themselves giving Gore one more chance to tango. He is the number one anti-Hillary Contender. He has a high-profile issue like global warming on which to base his campaign and many will view him as being correct from the start regarding his opposition to the war in Iraq. The question is, does he want it?

John Edwards
Who

The 2004 Democratic nominee for Vice President and one-term Senator from North Carolina, Edwards has spent more time in Iowa than any other Contender. A former trial lawyer, Edwards has positioned himself as the Contender who will run on a populist message.

Most polls show him with an early lead in Iowa which will make him a big target of the other Contenders going forward.

What

As Democrats strengthened their power in the Northeast and made gains in the Midwest and Mountain states in the 2006 mid-terms, the South remained a stronghold for the GOP. As a Southerner, Edwards might be able to bring into play a Southern state that could tip the election in favor of Democrats. Also, history shows that the last two Democratic Presidents were from the South.

Where

Edwards has been running for the 2008 nomination since John Kerry conceded in 2004. He has remained active on the speaking circuit, both he and his wife released new books and he was a strong campaigner for Democrats running in the 2006 mid-terms.

When/Will

Edwards will be one of the first to declare in order to maintain his early lead in the Iowa and New Hampshire polls. Once/if Hillary, Barack or Gore jump in, some of the oxygen will be sucked out of his campaign but if he stays consistent in his populist message, he still should be a factor in the race. If he remains competitive after Iowa and New Hampshire, when the primaries move South, he can make a strong move for the nomination.

Why

Edwards is confident that his message will resonate with voters and exit polls from the 2006 mid-terms showed that many voters are looking for a return to basic values from their leaders in government. As a former trial lawyer, Edwards has proven that he is a fighter for the little guy, the underdog, against the big and powerful. It's a theme that he will continue to use.

How

It may be difficult for Edwards to knock off challengers who possess much more experience than he does. As a one-term Senator, both he and Barack Obama possess the least amount of public service of the Democratic Contenders. However, that might be an advantage, especially if things are going better on the ground in Iraq. But if Iraq is still a long hard slog, voters might be looking for candidates with more foreign policy experience.

Wesley Clark
Who

Wesley Clark is a retired U.S. Army four-star General. He was the Supreme Allied Commander in Europe for NATO from 1997 to 2000, during which time he commanded Operation Allied Force in Kosovo. Clark is a graduate of West Point, was awarded a Rhodes scholarship to Oxford University and is a recipient of the Presidential Medal of Freedom. He previously ran for the Presidency in 2004.

What

Military experience, pure and simple, is Clark's greatest asset as a Presidential Contender. The last two Presidents have lacked that type of experience which has been clearly evident in the military decisions they have made. Clark has been extremely critical of the war in Iraq. "This is the first time that I've seen this country manipulated into war through deception of the American people," Clark has said.

Where

Clark's military service and previous Presidential campaign have given him the exposure any Contender needs and he is also a favorite of the "Netroots" which were so instrumental in the early success of Howard Dean during his campaign for President in 2004. Netroot campaigns were very active for Democratic candidates in the 2006 mid-term elections, most notably helping Ned Lamont defeat Joe Lieberman in the Connecticut primary although Lieberman would go on to win the general election.

When/Will

Early polling shows Clark lagging far behind other Presidential Contenders, but if the situation in Iraq and Afghanistan continues to go poorly, a "Draft Wesley Clark" campaign might go into full speed, much like it did in 2004. Clark, with the help of the netroots and George Soros, who has been a major contributor to Clark's candidacy, would have no problem raising campaign funds if/when he decided to jump in the race.

Why

Whereas John McCain's military service gives him an advantage in the field of Republican Contenders, Wesley Clark's service does the same for him in the Democratic field. Unlike John Kerry, Clark's service won't put him on the political defensive and while McCain has called for more troops in Iraq, Clark has called for an orderly withdrawal which puts him more in line with the majority of the American public.

How

Because of Iraq, Clark has a much better chance of getting the nomination in 2008. If he's truly committed he can raise the funds necessary to compete but he must find a way to better connect with the voters. His ideas and passion seem to get lost between the time when the words leave his mouth and make it to the voter's ears. America may want her next President to be Eisenhower-like and Clark certainly fits that to a tee.

Joe Biden
Who

Joe Biden has been a U.S. Senator since he was born (actually, since 1973) and is currently serving his sixth term. He has been Chairman of the Judiciary and Foreign Relations Committees and he previously ran for the Presidency in 1988 before withdrawing after it was discovered he had plagiarized a speech from British Labour Party leader Neil Kinnock.

What

In addition to being one of the nation's longest serving Senators, Biden claims an important leadership position in the Democratic Party and he's well respected in the GOP. He's a Moderate who has strong views that are respected on both sides of the aisle regarding ways to get U.S. troops out of Iraq. He has the experience that would make him attractive to a cross-section of voters.

Where

The public knows Biden to be a strong critic of the Bush administration and he appears regularly on the Sunday talk shows which raises his profile. Although he's critical of the current administration, he presents ideas for finding solutions that have been highly praised.

When/Will

Biden has already declared his candidacy and has been making the rounds in Iowa and New Hampshire. With Democrats now in leadership in the Senate, Biden has been instrumental in working with the

White House and all of Congress in developing the best options for ending the war in Iraq.

Why

Biden also has been down this road before and it has been long enough for him to again find the desire to make one last attempt. He thought about and decided not to run in 2004, and he possesses the type of foreign policy experience voters feel will be mandatory in their next Commander In Chief.

How

Biden's foreign policy experience is the key to any chance he has of winning the Presidency. He will be an integral part of any compromise between the White House and the Senate as it pertains to solutions about Iraq, Iran, Syria and North Korea. He has more experience than any other Democratic Contender and if he can ever learn to smile, he has a chance to upset some of the bigger names.

Barack Obama
Who

The junior Senator from Illinois, Barack Obama was elected to the Senate in November 2004 and has become, after Hillary Clinton, the most recognizable Democrat considering a run for the Presidency. Obama delivered the keynote address at the 2004 Democratic National Convention and during the 2006 mid-term elections, no Democrat, including Bill Clinton, was more sought out to campaign with Democrats around the country.

What

Obama has shot to the top of most Democratic Presidential polls. Only Hillary Clinton polls higher, but she also carries a higher negative rating than does Obama. Wherever Obama has traveled, he has electrified Democrats, Independents and even some Republicans. There is a sense that in a wide open primary like 2008, Obama has a solid chance to catch fire early and roll to the nomination.

Where

No Contender, Democrat or Republican, has received as much public attention as Obama. He has also yet to receive the full force of public scrutiny that will go along with any race for the Presidency. The obvious question in the minds of many is whether the country is ready to elect a Black candidate to the nation's highest office?

When/Will

Like Hillary Clinton, Obama can wait until late in the game to declare his candidacy. If he chose to run, he would have very little problem raising campaign funds. He would be the Contender most likely to raise significant sums in a grassroots fashion, much like Howard Dean accomplished with the internet during his failed run in 2004.

Why

Obama is a fresh face and he campaigns from the Center of the political spectrum. His message is meant to appeal to a broad swath of voters and his desire to see government act in a more bipartisan fashion is shared by many Americans. Like John F. Kennedy in 1960, Obama has captured the attention of the nation.

How

While Obama is an exciting figure, he has only served in the Senate since January, 2005. His lack of experience will be an issue, as will his race. Whether or not his personality will be strong enough to counteract his limited resume will be a major question. It is, however, hard to dismiss the enthusiasm he brought to the campaign trail in 2006. If he can do the same in a run for President, he may not get the nomination but the second slot on the ticket is a real possibility.

Tom Vilsack
Who

Tom Vilsack is the two-term Governor of Iowa. He previously served in the Iowa State Senate and was Mayor of Mount Pleasant, Iowa. Vilsack was the first Democrat to declare his candidacy late in 2006 and is viewed as a long shot to get the Democratic nomination.

What

Vilsack was the first Democrat in thirty years to be elected Governor in Iowa. He is well respected by Democrats and Republicans and is viewed as a Centrist. With Iowa being the first test in the campaign, a strong showing, specifically a win, by Vilsack could launch his campaign from unknown to well-known overnight.

Where

Not many voters outside of the Midwest know a great deal about Vilsack. He is a passable stump speaker and he has a true, only in America life story of "Success over adversity" that will rival any other Contender, Democrat or Republican.

When/Will

Vilsack is already out on the campaign trail and he needs to be. Once voters get a chance to see who he is and what he has to offer, many will be moved by what he brings to the table. His chances for success should rise accordingly.

Why

George W. Bush moved from Governor to President. Bill Clinton moved from Governor to President. Ronald Reagan moved from Governor to President. Jimmy Carter moved from Governor to President. Senators don't win the Presidency, Governors do. Vilsack is a Governor. Who's to say it can't happen?

How

Vilsack doesn't have to win in Iowa, but it sure wouldn't hurt. A top three finish still keeps him in the hunt. He is a Centrist and like Bill Clinton when he was the Governor of Arkansas, Vilsack is the current Chairman of the Democratic Leadership Council. Vilsack has the chance to be one of the surprise Contenders in the race for President. Unlike other candidates, he won't have the baggage of initially supporting the war in Iraq to carry around with him. Vilsack and his wife Christie were very influential in John Kerry's comeback win in Iowa in 2004 and if Kerry decides not to run, as he probably should, Vilsack will have some IOU's to call in.

Top-Tier Republican Contenders

"America's culture is also defined by the fact that we are a religious people. We recognize our God not only in our Declaration of Independence, but even in our currency. And we are also unique in that we recognize that the family is the fundamental building block of American society."
—Mitt Romney

Conventional wisdom says John McCain and Rudy Giuliani are the frontrunners in the race for the Republican nomination and most polls support that. But a struggle is underway within the GOP as to the direction it needs to head if it wants victory in 2008. Voters in 2006 sent a message to Republican leaders and that message was, "We're not very happy with you and we're more than willing to give the Democrats a shot."

Where does the GOP go from here? More conservative? Less conservative? McCain may be a frontrunner but he has prominent detractors within the Party. Giuliani, while well-liked, supports gay rights, abortion rights and gun control. Are Republican primary voters really going to coalesce behind a candidate with those beliefs?

Now, let's take a quick look at the Republicans who are thinking of jumping into the race for President:

John McCain
Who

John McCain is the senior Senator from Arizona, having served since 1987. He was held a prisoner of war in Vietnam for five years after his plane was shot down by an anti-aircraft missile. He previously ran for the Presidency in 2000, losing the nomination to George Bush after a brutal and ugly campaign.

What

After his loss to Bush, McCain has, as he said he would, remained loyal to the Republican Party and many see him as the GOP's best chance to retain the White House. At times he has found himself at odds with the Religious Right yet that has made him attractive to Independents and some Democrats, which is necessary if the GOP has any chance of holding onto the White House in 2008.

Where

Along with Rudy Giuliani, McCain is the highest profile Republican in the race for President. The public and press have come to see him as a "Maverick," not afraid to take positions that are unpopular. Many view him as an Independent who happens to be a Republican but he has made a concerted effort to move much further to the political Right as he mounts his bid for the Presidency for he knows full well he needs the GOP base to win the nomination.

When/Will

Most assume that McCain will enter the race and like most frontrunners, he can wait until relatively late to do so. He will have no difficulty raising additional funds to add to his already large war chest and he has firm commitments from Republican donors who were instrumental to George Bush in 2000.

Why

McCain is a war hero and has positioned himself as a candidate with the necessary foreign policy experience to get the country out of Iraq with victory and to also deal with other world threats including Iran, Syria and North Korea. His ability to attract votes across Party lines would make him difficult to defeat in a general election.

How

If McCain can make it out of the primaries, the Democrats may not be able to front a candidate that could beat him. He appeals to moderate Republicans, moderate Democrats and Independents which is basically all that he needs to win the Presidency. If, however, McCain continues to move Right in his effort to shore up the Republican base, it may turn away some of those Moderate voters he needs. His call for an increase in troop strength in Iraq, after an election in 2006 that showed most Americans want the opposite, could also hurt his chances.

Rudy Giuliani
Who

Rudy Giuliani is the former two-term Republican Mayor of New York City who became known as "America's Mayor" after the terrorist attacks on the World Trade Center on September 11th, 2001. He is currently Chairman and CEO of Giuliani Partners LLC, a security consulting company he founded in 2002.

What

In many early polls, Giuliani leads McCain. Giuliani is credited with turning New York around by getting the city's fiscal house in order, reducing crime and making the city more popular with tourists than ever before. Giuliani was overwhelmingly elected and re-elected as a Republican in a city that is strongly Democratic.

Where

Giuliani is one of the most popular public figures in the country. During the 2006 mid-term elections, he was highly desired on the campaign trail by Republican candidates. He appeals to voters across Party lines which, like McCain, would make him very popular in a general election but not necessarily the primaries.

When/Will

Giuliani needs to decide if he has a legitimate chance of winning the nomination or if it's better to lie low and position himself for the number two spot on a ticket. Being able to pair a Moderate with a Conservative on the Republican ticket could look very appealing to many voters.

Why

Giuliani is still viewed as a hero and, like McCain, if he makes it out of the primaries as the Republican nominee, there may not be anyone on the Democratic side that could beat him. Voters in 2006 told politicians that they want the pendulum to move back to the middle and Giuliani could even be considered left of middle.

How

It is unlikely Giuliani can win the Republican nomination. Conservative voters would not be able to overlook his liberal record on gun control, abortion and gay rights. It is also difficult to see religious conservatives support a ticket with Giuliani as the Vice Presidential nominee. Giuliani winning the Republican nomination would be one of the greatest political feats ever.

Sam Brownback
Who

Sam Brownback was first elected Kansas Senator in a special election in 1996 to replace Bob Dole who had resigned his seat to seek the Presidency. Since then, Brownback has been re-elected twice, the last time in 2004 after receiving nearly seventy percent of the popular vote.

What

Along with former Pennsylvania Senator Rick Santorum, Brownback is considered one of the staunchest social conservatives in Congress. He opposes same-sex marriage, abortion and pornography. With Santorum most likely out of the Presidential sweepstakes because of his defeat in 2006, Brownback, along with Mike Huckabee, is viewed as a dark horse conservative alternative to McCain and Giuliani.

Where

While not a household name, Brownback is well respected by Conservatives within the Republican Party. He is vocal in his opposition to embryonic stem cell research, which was a huge issue in the 2006 mid-terms, but he supports the use of cord blood stem cells for research and treatment.

When/Will

Brownback, like most of the lesser-known candidates, needs to declare early in order to build name recognition. He has been to Iowa and New Hampshire to speak and religious activists within the GOP, including Christian Coalition founder Pat Robertson, view a potential Brownback candidacy positively.

Why

Brownback, for social and religious Conservatives within the Republican Party, is everything that John McCain and Rudy Giuliani are not. Brownback converted from Protestant to Catholic in 2002 and he will be viewed as more acceptable to Christian Conservatives than the Mormon Mitt Romney. If Brownback runs, he can make the case that he and Mike Huckabee are the true Conservatives running for the Republican nomination.

How

While McCain, Giuliani and Romney might have problems convincing Republican base voters that they understand their issues, Brownback will not. If he and Huckabee both enter the race they will be fighting for many of the same votes, but a single entry from these two could make for an interesting primary race.

Mike Huckabee
Who

Two-term Governor of Arkansas, Mike Huckabee in 1998 received the largest percentage of votes for a Republican seeking statewide office in Arkansas history. Huckabee originally was sworn in as Governor in 1996 after Democratic Governor Jim Guy Tucker resigned after being convicted in the Whitewater scandal.

What

Huckabee is a former Baptist minister and on social issues is to the political Right of McCain and Giuliani, the early frontrunners. Huckabee, Sam Brownback and Mitt Romney are attempting to stake their claim to religious conservatives. Huckabee and Brownback would seem to have an advantage due to the question of how Romney's Mormon faith will play with evangelicals.

Where

Like another former Governor from Arkansas who went on to become President, Huckabee is not well known nationally. What is most known about him is his amazing personal weight loss. After being diagnosed with diabetes in 2003, Huckabee proceeded to lose one hundred and ten pounds through exercise and diet.

When/Will

Huckabee has already made the obligatory trips to many of the early primary states, including New Hampshire. While political pundits have his potential candidacy on their radar screens, Huckabee needs to enter the race early in 2007 to gain name recognition and cut into the lead that McCain, Giuliani and Romney have in the early polls.

Why

Many religious conservatives feel that the Bush administration has been a disappointment in addressing issues important to them and Huckabee, like Brownback, might be able to separate himself from the rest of the GOP pack by campaigning on those issues.

How

Huckabee can win by using the successful strategy of divide and conquer. For him, the more GOP contenders in the race, the better, especially if Sam Brownback does not run. McCain and Giuliani will always be viewed with suspicion by many religious conservatives while Romney's Mormon faith is still a huge wild card. Huckabee is strong on the stump and his successful weight loss helps him to campaign on the important issue of health care in America.

Mitt Romney
Who

Former Governor of Massachusetts and CEO of the 2002 Salt Lake City Winter Olympics, Mitt Romney may be the biggest wild card in the Republican Party. Romney is a staunch Conservative who was elected in one of the most liberal states in the country. He has been well-received by Conservatives with prominent voices in the GOP, including those at the *National Review* and the Heritage Foundation.

What

Romney's success in a blue state, his good looks and his conservative values make him a candidate that Republican voters will have to look at closely. The eight hundred pound gorilla in the room, however, is the fact that Romney is a Mormon. No one quite knows how that will play with certain voters around the country. Romney may also have some difficulty explaining his previous support of a woman's right to choose an abortion, gay rights and his backing of embryonic stem cell research.

Where

Romney's no longer under the radar and he has been getting as much press as McCain and Giuliani. He has faithfully been making the rounds in Iowa and New Hampshire. He is a strong speaker and as his views on national issues become more known, his profile grows.

When/Will

Romney has been unofficially on the campaign trail for some time now. He needs to continue to build name recognition and he also must deal with the fact that his Lieutenant Governor was beaten badly in the Massachusetts Governor's race in 2006, leaving some to believe he abandoned her in pursuit of his own agenda. Being from Massachusetts makes him a strong Contender in New Hampshire.

Why

Romney is positioning himself as a hard-line fiscal and social Conservative. Many in the GOP are looking for someone that can also challenge Democrats in the Northeast, West and Mountain states where Republicans have begun to lose ground and Romney may be that type of Contender.

How

As Barack Obama and Hillary Clinton bring the issues of race and gender front and center, Romney does the same with religion. No one quite knows how his being Mormon will be received by Christian Conservatives. Also, experience will be a question in that Romney is a one-term Governor. New Hampshire will be the key for him. He must win there to prove he's a viable Contender.

Newt Gingrich
Who

As the 58th United States Speaker of the House and co-author of the "Contract With America," Newt Gingrich was the leader of the Republican Revolution which triumphed in the House of Representatives in 1994. For the next twelve years, Republicans would hold onto the majority in the House and during Gingrich's tenure, which lasted until 1999, he remained a thorn in the side as well as a successful working partner with President Bill Clinton.

What

More than any other Republican Contender, Gingrich identifies with the political legacy of Ronald Reagan and he believes that the GOP has forgotten the lessons of the former President. With embarrassing losses in the 2006 mid-terms, many in the Republican Party are beginning to agree with him yet they're not sure Gingrich is the best messenger to help bring back Reagan Conservatives to the fold.

Where

Gingrich is still remembered by the public for his success in the 90's but also for the ethics charges that were brought against him and his fall from grace: Losing the Speaker's gavel and his eventual resignation from the House. He, like Hillary Clinton, is seen by the opposition as a polarizing figure and he has high negative ratings in most polling.

When/Will

Gingrich did in 2005 what most potential candidates do: He wrote a book. With "Winning the Future: A 21st Century Contract with America," Gingrich hopes to build on not only his previous success but that of the Republican Party during the Reagan years. After the bitter losses in the 2006 mid-terms, the GOP wants nothing more than to regain power in 2008 and Gingrich believes that by getting voters to remember Reagan, he can find success.

Why

Gingrich will be positioned far to the right and even though voters may not think he can win, a vote for Gingrich could be a vote for the direction that Republicans want the Party to head. He won't do well with moderate Republicans and Independents, but for the hard-liners, Gingrich will resonate.

How

Gingrich can't win the nomination, but he could take some votes away from McCain and Romney. Gingrich is a strong public speaker and he has the ability to stir the base. He's not a potential Vice President, but a strong showing in the primaries might be sufficient to get him some prime time at the Republican National Convention.

Chuck Hagel
Who

A United States Senator since 1997, Chuck Hagel is a Vietnam War veteran who earned the Purple Heart. Hagel has been widely critical of the Bush administration regarding their handling of the war in Iraq. He has also chastised the Republican Party for failing to live up to its core principals of fiscal responsibility and small government.

What

Like McCain, Hagel's service in Vietnam gives him certain credibility on issues of national defense. He was one of the first Republicans to come out in public and break with his President, specifically Vice President Cheney's belief that the Iraqi insurgency was in its "last throes." The 2006 mid-term results proved that even Republicans were growing tired of the Iraq conflict and Hagel was well ahead of the curve within his Party in seeing that.

Where

Hagel doesn't have the public persona that others in the GOP possess, but he sits on four Senate committees and is a regular visitor on the Sunday talk show circuit. Although a Republican, and conservative, Hagel is viewed much more as a libertarian which may be a positive in a Party looking to find its way back to the political center.

When/Will

If he declares, Hagel needs to get out on the campaign trail very early. He has already made visits to Iowa and New Hampshire to test the water, but he needs to refine his stump speech. He is certainly not the most dynamic speaker in the bunch, but if his positions regarding the war and the future of his Party can reach enough ears, voters may start to take a closer look.

Why

Like McCain, Hagel wore his country's uniform, so it will be hard to question his national defense credentials even though he and McCain have differing views on how the country needs to go forward in Iraq. As a moderate Republican, he could be an attractive candidate to a large number of voters in a general election.

How

The larger the Republican field, the better for Hagel. Looking at the top-tier Republicans, Hagel is probably the most Centrist. If he can manufacture some excitement in his campaign and if he can raise enough money to stick around for a while, he just might have a chance. Without question, if he was interested, he would be a perfect Vice Presidential candidate.

George Pataki
Who

The Governor of New York State, George Pataki is the longest serving sitting Governor in America. He became Governor in 1995 and he has never lost a political campaign in his career. He was mentioned as a possible running mate for George Bush in 2000.

What

Pataki, like Giuliani, has been a successful Republican in a blue state like New York mainly by remaining liberal on social issues like abortion. He has been a consistent tax cutter and is a strong proponent of privatization of state entities. Although his popularity has waned somewhat, he would still put New York's electoral votes in play as a Republican nominee.

Where

Although he doesn't possess the star power of Rudy Giuliani, Pataki was credited with bringing the 2004 Republican National Convention to New York City. Coming three years after September 11th, 2001, the event was a success for the GOP as well as the city. Pataki's profile was raised and talk of a run for the Presidency in 2008 began.

When/Will

Pataki needs to decide if he wants to keep his perfect campaign record intact because the odds of him winning the nomination are small. He also dealt with some serious health issues in 2006 which may factor into his decision. He will probably decide well before January, 2008, if he has any desire to run.

Why

Pataki is a skilled campaigner and is viewed positively within the GOP but it's doubtful that would be enough to knock off the bigger names. Giuliani overshadows him with anything having to do with 9/11. There doesn't seem to be much that would give reason to believe Pataki could win.

How

Pataki can't win the nomination but he willed be viewed as a potential running mate. Whether he could bring New York State into play as the second on a ticket is questionable, but he could certainly be a strong balance if the top off the ticket was a true social conservative.

Pretenders

al so-ran

-noun

1. *Sports.*

   a. *(in a race) a contestant who fails to win or to place among the first three finishers.*

   b. *an athlete or team whose performance in competition is rarely, if ever, a winning or near-winning one.*

2. *Informal. a person who loses a contest, election, or other competition.*

3. *Informal. a person who attains little or no success: For every great artist there are a thousand also-rans.*

"It is true that Mr. Lincoln signed the Emancipation Proclamation, after which there was a commitment to give 40 acres and a mule. That's where the argument, to this day, of reparations starts. We never got the 40 acres. We went all the way to Herbert Hoover, and we never got the 40 acres. We didn't get the mule. So we decided we'd ride this donkey as far as it would take us."

—Al Sharpton

While the race for President is a serious endeavor, it's always entertaining to watch the candidates that have no chance of winning get the opportunity to speak to America. Over the last few Presidential election cycles, with a Republican in the White House, we've had the pleasure of watching a plethora of Democrats perform at the candidate forums. No candidate is as fun to watch as the Reverend Al Sharpton.

Just a few of the great one-liners from the Rev:

> *"George Bush giving tax cuts is like Jim Jones giving Kool-Aid. It tastes good but it'll kill you."*

> *"I understand deficit spending. I was born in deficit spending."*

> *"I wanted to say to Governor Dean, don't be hard on yourself about hooting and hollering. If I had spent the money you did and got 18 percent, I'd still be in Iowa hooting and hollering."*

> *"Crime is going down everywhere but in the New York City Police Department."*

> *"I'm not interested in being Archie Bunker. I'm looking forward to becoming George Bush."*

> *"Young lady, it is time for the Christian Right to meet the right Christians."*

While he may be glib and funny, "Also-Rans" like Al Sharpton and Dennis Kucinich serve an important purpose in a Presidential race: They help keep the legitimate Contenders honest.

With a wide open field in both the Democrat and Republican Parties, the candidates that can't win will play to their respective liberal and conservative bases and make Clinton, McCain, Edwards, Giuliani and the rest of them tackle issues they might prefer not to touch.

Then maybe, just maybe, if not a Sharpton or Kucinich or Tancredo, one of those also-rans might break through and become a legitimate Contender, the guy nobody thought about or heard of before. The Jimmy Carter. It's doubtful that will happen in 2008 with so many big names in the race, but one never knows, does one?

Let's take a quick look at the lower-tier candidates who might jump into the race and see if they have any chance at all:

Jeb Bush

It's unlikely that anyone with the last name "Bush" is going to get anywhere near the Oval Office for a very long time, unless it's just for a quick visit. Jeb Bush may prove to be the most intelligent Bush son but he can thank his older brother George for making him have to wait until at least 2012 to even think about running for President.

Bill Richardson

The Governor of New Mexico just might jump into the fray. He brings a great deal of executive experience to the game and his Hispanic heritage is definitely a positive factor. He won't win but a Vice Presidential spot is a real possibility.

Tommy Thompson

Former Wisconsin Governor. Former Secretary of Health and Human Services. Soon to be former 2008 Presidential candidate. No shot at all.

Rick Santorum

After the drubbing Santorum took at the hands of Bob Casey in the Pennsylvania Senate race, he might as well say goodbye to any Presidential aspirations. Pennsylvania voters got sick of his holier-than-thou act and they're a pretty conservative bunch to start with. Santorum has plenty of time now to stay in the house and home school his kids.

Ed Rendell

Speaking of Pennsylvania, the Democratic Pennsylvania Governor demolished opponent Lynn Swann to retain his seat. "Fast Eddie" is basically unbeatable in his state. 2008 may not be the time for him to make a run at the Presidency but if a knock came at the door for the second spot, he'd jump. If he doesn't go this time he'll definitely be in for 2012 if a Democrat isn't already there.

Condi Rice

Rice scores generally well in most polls and probably has the highest approval rating of anyone serving in the Bush administration, which may not be saying much. Everyone's dream scenario is Hillary vs. Condi. Unfortunately, it will have to remain a dream. Her fingerprints, along with Bush, Cheney and Rumsfeld, are all over Iraq. What, she's going to resign and run for President as that country continues to spiral downward? Not gonna happen.

Chris Dodd

Connecticut Senator since 1981. Backed the losing guy in the 2006 Connecticut Democratic primary and then followed that up by backing the losing guy in the Connecticut general election. Nice guy himself, but no shot.

Tom Tancredo

A staunch critic of illegal immigration, Tancredo is one of those candidates that could make life very difficult for a guy like John McCain. Tancredo has been a fierce opponent of Bush's proposed immigration policies, which Tancredo and many others call amnesty, and which is supported by McCain. The issue was heavily debated during the 2006 mid-term elections and will continue to hurt McCain with the Republican base. Tancredo is not who John McCain wants to stand next to at a Republican candidate's forum. Tancredo will most likely run even though he can't win and cause McCain to have nightmares.

Al Sharpton

He's funny, glib, colorful and polarizing. He's also one of the smartest people up on stage when he's there with his fellow Democrats and it would be a shame if he didn't run. Of course he's got no shot, but who cares. That's not the point. Keep them honest Al, keep them honest.

Tom Ridge

Former Governor of Pennsylvania and Secretary of Homeland Security, you don't hear much from Ridge these days. After leaving the Bush administration at the end of 2004, Ridge has kept busy working in the private sector. He's been on a couple of short lists: For Bush's Vice President and Secretary of Defense. He probably won't run but he would be an interesting candidate if he did.

Dennis Kucinich

Like the Reverend Al, Kucinich obviously has no chance but he would keep his fellow Democrats on their toes, especially when it comes to the war in Iraq. All of those Senators that voted to give Bush authorization for the war dread getting a verbal lashing from Kucinich. He could be Hillary Clinton's nightmare at a candidate's forum.

Tom Daschle

Like Rick Santorum and George Allen, losing your Senate seat isn't a great way to jump-start your Presidential campaign. No shot, but that still may not prevent him from trying. He's been making stops on the speaking circuit so he's definitely thinking about it.

George Allen

Allen lost any chance of reaching the White House, as well as holding onto his Virginia Senate seat, with the use of one word: Maccaca.

Eventually, all of America would have figured out what Virginians finally did in 2006: George Allen isn't the brightest bulb in the lamp and is certainly ill-suited to be President of the United States.

Colin Powell

Even if his wife would support a bid by the former Secretary of State, his time in the Bush cabinet has made him damaged goods. Who can ever forget his speech at the United Nations arguing in favor of military action in Iraq? Powell will never forget or maybe ever forgive himself.

Mark Sanford

If Sanford runs, hopefully he'll remember to bring his voter registration card so he'll be able to cast a ballot for himself in the South Carolina primary. Probably not in 2008 but don't count him out for 2012 if a Democrat is in the White House.

Duncan Hunter

Former chairman of the House Armed Services Committee, Hunter and Tommy Thompson must have had the same person whisper in their ears telling them to run. Nothing more than a vanity exercise. No chance.

Who the Democrats and Republicans SHOULD Nominate

"Somebody gets to be smart and somebody gets to be dumb. If we win, it'll be because of the president. And if we lose, it'll be because of me."

—Karl Rove

On Election Day, November 7, 2006, Karl Rove still firmly believed Republicans would continue to control both the House of Representatives and the Senate. In one interview with a reporter, it was pointed out to Rove that in all the polling data that was being compiled, the math just didn't add up. The GOP was going to lose big.

Rove responded by saying that he had *"The math,"* and his math was telling him that Republicans would hold onto their majorities. He was very wrong. Rove and President Bush would go to sleep that night suffering the worst defeat in their political lives. Although neither of them was on the ballot, the voting public and political pundits saw the Democratic victory as a repudiation of the President and "Rovian" political philosophy.

Exit polling confirmed the public's unhappiness. The top three reasons given as why voters wanted to see a change in leadership in Congress were:

1. Dissatisfaction with President Bush's overall performance.

2. Dissatisfaction with the war in Iraq.

3. Dissatisfaction with the overall sense of corruption in the Republican controlled Congress.

Voters were fed up and Republican Senators and Representatives who were thought to be safe for re-election began falling like dominos election night. The next day, Bush called it a "thumpin." He also tried to put some spin on the results by saying that the races were close. A few thousand votes here, a few thousand votes there and the evening could have turned out much differently.

While that may be true, if you look at the total number of votes cast in every contest nationwide, 53% of votes cast were for Democrats and 47% were for Republicans. After Bush defeated Kerry in 2004 with 52% of the popular vote he called it a mandate. This was a mandate as well and Bush and Rove knew it.

Now it's time to look forward to Election 2008. With the race for President the integral part of that election, the Democrat and Republican Contenders are going to be the most important factor in determining if Democrats can keep their momentum through another election cycle or if the Republicans can stop the bleeding and gain back some lost ground.

For each Party, the eventual nominees will help determine:

1. If the GOP will retain or if the Democrats can regain the White House.

2. If the Democrats retain control of both houses of Congress. While the Democrats could lose seats in the House, it's unlikely the Republicans can regain the majority after just one election cycle. In the Senate, as the map looks now, the Republicans will have even more seats at risk in 2008 than in 2006. It would be a major success for the GOP if it came out of the 2008 election where they stand now, just two seats down.

3. Control of Governorships and State Legislatures. Democrats made significant gains in both areas and they now hold twenty-eight Governorships compared to twenty-two for the Republicans.

Much is at stake, so the question now is which Contender is best positioned to help their respective Party achieve its objectives? Is it a new face? Is it an old hand? Is it a Governor, Senator? Who SHOULD the Democrats and Republicans nominate?

First, let's look at who should not get the nod and we'll start with the Democrats:

Hillary Clinton

Hillary Clinton won't win a general election. Hillary Clinton will have difficulty winning the Democratic nomination. Her negative ratings are far too high for her to have any chance of knocking off a top-tier Republican, especially McCain or Giuliani. Although she's tried to move to the political center, there are too many voters that find her polarizing and although her husband is as popular as ever, it just doesn't rub off on her. Democrats should not nominate her.

John Kerry

Kerry had his chance in 2004 and he blew it. His mouth continues to get him into trouble and voters view him as weak. In another general election, he would get a lower percentage of votes than he received in 2004. He shouldn't enter the primary races at all.

John Edwards

Edwards doesn't have the experience or stature for the country to feel comfortable handing over the reins to him. He's got an interesting life story that he weaves for audiences to full effect and he's good on the stump but he just doesn't pass one important test: He doesn't "Feel"

Presidential. He almost still seems too young for the job. A top-tier Republican would beat him in a general election.

Joe Biden

Biden has the experience, he has strong foreign policy credentials, and he's been down this road before. That might be his problem. The circumstances of his last failed run may hang over him. He's a competent speaker but he isn't going to blow anybody away on the stump. He would be a tougher challenge for a Republican in the general election but he would still come up short.

Barack Obama

Obama is a star. He's brings excitement wherever he goes as was seen in the 2006 mid-terms. He's as popular, if not more popular right now, than Bill Clinton in the Democratic Party. But like John Edwards, he just doesn't have the experience and the question will be asked, even if many preferred not to, if the country is ready to elect a Black president? Do the Democrats want to take that chance in 2008 and find out that America wasn't?

Wesley Clark

Wesley Clark certainly has the type of military experience that many Americans would want their next Commander In Chief to possess. The last two President's lack of significant, or any, military service coupled with the military decisions that those Presidents made have created distrust between the White House and the Pentagon. Clark has a military resume unmatched by any Contender, Democrat or Republican. You also can't overlook the support Clark garners from the netroots. However, netroot support won't be large enough to bring him victory in the Democratic primaries or the general election.

Tom Vilsack

Vilsack is the second best option for the Democrats to nominate. Yes, right now he's a long shot and he's well under the radar, but he's the former Iowa Governor and he would certainly get a nice bounce by winning the Iowa caucuses, although that's no guarantee. He's moderate in his political views. He's been a two-term Governor in a state that hadn't elected a Democrat for Governor in over three decades. He brings red state America in the Midwest into play for the Democrats. He's been Chair of the Democratic Leadership Council, just like Bill Clinton. His life story, including adoption as an orphan and a lifetime struggle dealing with his mother's alcoholism, will play well on the campaign trail. He's getting stronger on the stump and he looks and feels Presidential. Unlike Hillary Clinton, Kerry, Edwards and Biden, Vilsack, like Obama, doesn't have to defend voting to authorize President Bush to go to war in Iraq. With his geographical attractiveness, he would be a formidable challenge to any of the Republican Contenders. But, will his lack of foreign policy experience hurt him? Do voters want to give another Governor with limited foreign policy credentials another go in the White House after the debacle that is Iraq? Vilsack would be a solid choice but it may not be his time yet.

Al Gore

So, it looks like the Democrats need to go back a ways in the past for their best opportunity to take back the White House in the future because it lies with Al Gore. But does he want it? So far, the answer has been no, but it will be eight years since the last time Gore was in the ring and many see him as the best anti-Hillary candidate, the only one that could potentially stop Hillary from leading Democrats to defeat again in 2008.

How can Gore win? He certainly came close the last time in winning the popular vote. Looking at the electoral map, in 2008, he doesn't need Florida, which he wouldn't get anyway. Florida, as we saw in the 2006 mid-terms, is becoming much more of a solid red state. Gore's best chance to win the Presidency lies in finding ways to win in New Hampshire, Ohio, Colorado and Missouri, all states he lost in 2000.

Gore would likely hold onto the states he won in 2000 including Wisconsin and New Mexico, two states he won by the slimmest of margins. New Hampshire, Ohio (with a Democrat now as Governor), and Colorado are looking much bluer based on the mid-term results and are prime for Gore pickups. Missouri would still be a battleground and could swing either way.

Even if Gore lost Wisconsin, New Mexico and didn't flip Missouri, picking up New Hampshire, Ohio and Colorado, which looks very possible for Democrats, would give him 288 electoral votes. Florida is a non-factor and with the Hispanic vote disproportionately going in favor of Democrats in 2006, states like Arizona and Nevada now come into play, especially if Bill Richardson is the Vice Presidential nominee.

From an electoral perspective, the map looks much better for Gore. He's a known quantity. Many will see his opposition to the current war in Iraq as having been the right decision but he also voted in favor of the Gulf War in 1991 which many will also see as being right on. That gives him the political cover on Iraq Kerry could never get.

Al Gore gives Democrats their best chance to regain the White House. If he runs his Presidential campaign much like he has been running his campaign against global warming, Gore could exorcise the demons of the 2000 race when voters just couldn't get a handle on who this guy was. However, if he turns into "Robo-Gore," it could end badly once more.

Much like Nixon in 1968, this election could be Gore's comeback. It will be up to him to decide if he's ready, willing and able.

Now let's look at the Republicans:

George Pataki

Pataki is not someone the GOP should be looking at for the nomination but he definitely is going to be at the top of any nominee's Vice Presidential list. While it's still unlikely that he could help deliver New York State to the Republicans as the number two on a ticket, he would surely make Democrats have to spend more money there then they would like.

Mike Huckabee

While Huckabee could prove to be a darling of social and religious Conservatives, in a general election, that might hurt more than help. Voters in 2006 definitively moved towards the political center and Huckabee's strong religious faith will bring up the discussion of religion and its influence on government. Huckabee has publicly supported "Covenant Marriages" and his association with "Reclaim America for Christ Conferences" will raise some red flags.

Sam Brownback

With Rick Santorum most likely out of the race, Brownback picks up the baton as the most social and religious conservative in the group. While that may play well with base voters, it would be a disaster in the general election. Whether Brownback would also be viewed as too far right for the Vice Presidential spot is another issue for the eventual nominee.

Newt Gingrich

If Hillary Clinton is the bogeywoman for Republicans then Newt Gingrich is the bogeyman for Democrats. Gingrich's desire to run on the legacy of Ronald Reagan makes perfect sense but it just needs to be done by someone other than him. Voters will always remember Gingrich as a driving force behind the impeachment of Bill Clinton. He would be destroyed in a general election.

Rudy Giuliani

If Rudy Giuliani made it through the Republican primaries and won the GOP nomination, he would present very serious problems for a Democratic challenger. There's only one problem: Rudy Giuliani just might be further to the Left than anyone running on the Democratic side. There's no way he can win the Republican nomination. While Republicans are intent on holding onto the White House, GOP primary voters won't be able to hold their noses and vote for a candidate that's pro-choice, pro gay rights and pro gun control. It's not going to happen.

Mitt Romney

Romney's success as a conservative Republican in a blue state like Massachusetts might transfer to a general election, but it's unlikely. Also, much like Hillary Clinton has to deal with the gender issue and Barack Obama has to deal with the race issue, Romney has to deal with the religion issue. No one quite knows how that's going to play nationally, especially with Christian Conservatives who are openly suspicious of Mormons.

Chuck Hagel

Hagel is the second best option for the Republicans to nominate. Like Tom Vilsack, he's flying under the radar right now but his Nebraska roots make him a serious Contender to win the Iowa caucuses. Hagel was one of the first politicians in the GOP to come out and openly criticize the Bush administration's handling of Iraq. Hagel also criticized Karl Rove for calling Democrats unpatriotic and predicted that those types of comments would damage the GOP in the 2006 mid-term elections. He was right. Hagel, like Visack, is the type of Centrist politician that voters in both political Parties and Independents would support. The electorate has seen sixteen years of divisive politics and while politicians on either side may not be singing together around a campfire anytime soon, voters want steady, non-partisan leadership once elections are over. Chuck Hagel can deliver that and he would be a formidable challenge for the Democrats.

John McCain

If he can make it through the primaries, John McCain is the GOP's best chance to retain control of the White House. The Democrats will be hard-pressed to find a candidate that can appeal to Republicans, Independents and moderate-to-conservative Democrats like McCain will. The big problem for McCain will be getting primary voters in the Republican Party to give him the nomination.

Since 2000, after losing to George Bush, McCain and the Religious Right have had what could be called a bumpy relationship. It will be difficult, if not impossible, for a Republican to get the nomination without support from evangelicals. In 2000, Bush was able to turn the evangelical vote in his favor, specifically in the South Carolina primaries, which all but killed McCain's chances.

McCain has worked to mend those fences. In 2006, he gave the commencement address at Jerry Falwell's Liberty University and stated that Falwell was no longer the "Agent of intolerance" that McCain had described him to be in 2000. While that may have helped McCain's standing with evangelicals, it began the whispering among Moderates and Independents as to whether or not McCain was still the maverick many thought him to be.

McCain also has to deal with questions from the Republican base regarding the immigration legislation he coauthored with Ted Kennedy, which many see as amnesty. Immigration will still be a top issue in the 2008 race and McCain's stance puts him at odds with many in the GOP.

Like many candidates, McCain realizes that primaries are all about the base voters and the question for him will be if he's done enough bridge-building for those voters to give him their support? If not, a candidate like Chuck Hagel or Mike Huckabee may be more appealing to GOP voters.

Another issue McCain will have to address will be his age. If elected, he would be the oldest president ever to take the oath of office, almost two years older than Ronald Reagan.

Ultimately, McCain holds the GOP's best hope for getting at least four more years of Republican control of the White House. He, more than any other candidate in either Party, will draw a cross-section of voters that will be hard to beat in a general election. But there is no guarantee Republicans will even give him the chance.

Who Will Win

"I believe the most solemn duty of the American president is to protect the American people. If America shows uncertainty and weakness in this decade, the world will drift toward tragedy. This will not happen on my watch."
—George W. Bush

It's become increasingly clear that any resolution to the conflicts in Iraq and Afghanistan will have to be brokered by the next President of the United States, who will take the oath of office in January, 2009. Very few Americans, including the Neo-Conservative architects of the wars, expected the "Major combat operations" to last as long as they have.

On May 1st, 2003, aboard the USS Abraham Lincoln, President Bush stated that "In the battle of Iraq, the United States and our allies have prevailed. And now our coalition is engaged in securing and reconstructing that country." Those words of premature victory will reverberate in the ears of Americans for generations to come and will be a cautionary tale for the next person to sit in the Oval Office.

Which leads to the critical question: Who will be the next President of the United States? The pros and cons of each Contender and Pretender have been laid out in the previous chapters and we've analyzed which Contenders from each Party are best positioned to win the Presidency. Now, it's time to make final predictions as to who actually will be victorious.

It would be easy to look at the frontrunners in each Party and choose them as the eventual nominees but as you take a closer look at Hillary Clinton and John McCain, you recognize that each sits precariously atop the early polls. It could be that both can't go much higher while lesser-known candidates have no place to go but upward as the public gets to know more about them. Some in the Democratic Party just don't think Hillary Clinton can win a general election while some Republicans still see John McCain as less than a team player.

That's why this race is a wide open affair that is perfectly suited for Contenders that currently sit under the radar to come along and steal the nominations. That is just what is likely to occur.

So, let's begin by listing all the candidates that have been evaluated, starting with the Democrats:

Hillary Clinton

John Kerry

Al Gore

John Edwards

Wesley Clark

Joe Biden

Barack Obama

Tom Vilsack

Bill Richardson

Ed Rendell

Chris Dodd

Al Sharpton

Dennis Kucinich

Tom Daschle

First, the Pretenders are cut, and this is done with the knowledge that there always remains a slight chance that a Pretender could turn into a Contender, and that would certainly be embarrassing for those of us doing the predicting. Odds are pretty long for the Pretenders, but if there is one among the Democrats that has the potential to make a serious bid for the Presidency it would be Governor Bill Richardson.

That leaves the following eight, the original Democratic Contenders:

Hillary Clinton

John Kerry

Al Gore

John Edwards

Wesley Clark

Joe Biden

Barack Obama

Tom Vilsack

Next, remove the following Contenders: Hillary Clinton, John Kerry and Joe Biden. Kerry is removed from contention because, well, he's John Kerry. Never has someone dropped so far, so fast in American politics. Biden, while certainly qualified, seems to be old news. Hillary Clinton, of course, is the big cut here. Yes, she has the name, the money, the profile, but in the end, Democrats will come to one conclusion regarding Hillary Clinton: She is not Bill Clinton. She has two choices: Don't run or run and be defeated. Either way, Hillary Clinton will not get the Democratic nomination.

Remaining, there are:

Al Gore

John Edwards

Wesley Clark

Barack Obama

Tom Vilsack

Next cut: Barack Obama and Wesley Clark. Clark possesses all of the military credentials anyone could ask for yet he seems to have difficulty making that ultimate connection with voters. He also lacks the "Star" factor necessary to take that final step to the Presidency. Obama, on the other hand, reeks of it. So why won't Obama win? Sure, he's a rising star. He sits near the top of most early polls, running only behind Hillary. But Democratic voters will have reservations about one specific Obama attribute: Not his race, but his lack of experience. How can a Senator who is only midway through his first elected term get elected President? What an amazing feat it would be. Obama may very well be President one day but it will not be this time around.

Leaving us with the final three:

Gore

Edwards

Vislack

As was written in the previous chapter, an Al Gore candidacy may be the best opportunity the Democrats have to get back in the White House, but will Democrats give him another opportunity? What if he loses, again? The finger-pointing after another failed attempt would never end and with so many new, fresh Democratic Contenders vying for the nomination, do Democratic voters really want to, or need to, look to the past?

Edwards, like Obama, has the electrifying personality that can get a crowd of supporters revved up to full throttle but, like Obama, experience, or lack thereof, will be an issue for him. He only served one term in the Senate and since being a part of the losing Democratic ticket in 2004, all he's been doing is running full-time for 2008.

Tom Vilsack is the dark-horse candidate, the Governor from the small state of Iowa, the Chairman of the Democratic Leadership

Council. Although he's not even a shoo-in to win in his home state's caucuses, shown by the fact that he's running behind in early Iowa polls, Vilsack has personality, stature, and once voters get a look at him and listen to his story, he will become a viable candidate.

Tom Vilsack might be a long-shot, but he will win the Democratic nomination for President in 2008. He has been forefront in the resurgence of the Democratic Party in Iowa, a red state in the middle of red states that are critical to Democratic success in the race for the Presidency. He is a Centrist, which is key in a country that is moving rapidly to the center of the political spectrum. Finally, while not the rock star that Obama, Clinton and Edwards may be, Vilsack can get Republican and Moderate votes in a general election that those three would have much more difficulty corralling. For Democrats to win, they must think beyond the primaries and the flashing lights of Hillary and Obama. If they do, they will see that Tom Vilsack represents a more than solid chance for victory in 2008.

Now, the Republicans:

John McCain

Rudy Giuliani

Mike Huckabee

Mitt Romney

Newt Gingrich

Chuck Hagel

George Pataki

Jeb Bush

Tommy Thompson

Rick Santorum

Condi Rice

Tom Tancredo

Tom Ridge

Sam Brownback

George Allen

Colin Powell

Mark Sanford

Duncan Hunter

Again, the Pretenders are the first cut. For the Republicans, two of these Pretenders stand out as candidates that could move to the Contender stage if the right chips were to fall into place: Mark Sanford and Tom Ridge. Like Bill Richardson for the Democrats, both potentially could make some noise if they decided to jump in the race.

That leaves the following eight, the original Republican Contenders:

John McCain

Rudy Giuliani

Sam Brownback

Mike Huckabee

Mitt Romney

Newt Gingrich

Chuck Hagel

George Pataki

Next, remove the following Contenders: Rudy Giuliani, Newt Gingrich and George Pataki. Giuliani's left-leaning positions on abortion and gay rights generally exclude him from winning the Republican nomination while Gingrich's far right-leaning desires, like wanting to limit free speech by censoring the internet, an idea that would destroy any chance of the GOP getting back those Moderate voters it so desperately needs, knocks him out of the running. Pataki just seems to lack that "It" factor.

Remaining, we now have:

John McCain

Sam Brownback

Mike Huckabee

Mitt Romney

Chuck Hagel

Next to go: Sam Brownback and Chuck Hagel. Brownback will definitely find significant support from social and religious conservatives in the GOP, but in the end, there won't be enough votes to win the nomination and he would get pummeled in a general election if he got that far. Hagel, unfortunately, will be punished because he was one of the first GOP politicians to openly criticize the Bush administration's handling of the Iraq war. A true shame, because Hagel just might be the most thoughtful and intelligent of all the Republican Contenders, not just because of the independence he displayed by stepping up and castigating his President but for his ability to competently speak about where his Party has gone wrong and what it needs to do to get back on track. He would be a formidable challenger.

That leaves the final three of:

McCain

Romney

Huckabee

Since 2000, McCain has patiently waited his turn and he's tried to make peace with his detractors in the GOP. The problem for McCain is many of those detractors either don't want to make peace with him or don't trust him, and they never will. This will prove to be fatal for his chances to win the nomination.

Romney may prove to be the best funded and most strategic of all the Republican Contenders, but in the end, his Mormon roots may just be too much for some evangelicals to look past, especially when there are other Contenders that will make them feel they aren't taking a leap of faith, no pun intended. Like Hillary's gender and Obama's race, Romney's faith may not be the only factor that precludes him from winning the nomination, but to say that it wasn't a factor at all would be disingenuous.

Last man standing is Mike Huckabee. As Bill Clinton was before him, Huckabee is from Hope, Arkansas, and the Republican field is set up for him to see his way to the nomination.

Another long-shot, Mike Huckabee will win the Republican nomination for President in 2008. Huckabee's religious roots make him attractive to evangelicals who have at times felt abandoned by the current administration and who see no friend in either McCain or Giuliani. He is a fiscal and social conservative, the compassionate conservative which George W. Bush campaigned as but failed to deliver. Huckabee's conservatism makes him appealing to the Reaganites that Gingrich is courting. Finally, as a former Baptist preacher, Huckabee is a very strong orator on the stump and his personal victory over obesity is a story, when tied in with his campaign for health care reform, will be a winner as he campaigns throughout the country.

So, it will be Democratic Presidential Nominee Tom Vilsack versus Republican Presidential Nominee Mike Huckabee. Both are considered long-shots but as voters see more of them, it will become clear that both possess the two factors that are necessary to win in 2008: Electability and a relative clean slate. Whereas the majority of the voting public has already decided whether they like, trust or would vote for Hillary,

McCain, Kerry, Giuliani and all the rest, most have still yet to learn enough about Vilsack and Huckabee. When they do, Democrat and Republican voters will see that these two Contenders offer a strong chance for their respective Parties to win the 2008 Presidential election.

Who will win? In a race pitting Vilsack against Huckabee, Vilsack has the edge. Democrats are obviously experiencing the larger bounce from the 2006 mid-term elections and that should carry over into the Presidential and Congressional elections in 2008. Therefore, the predictions are that Tom Vilsack will be elected President of the United States, Democrats will increase their slight lead in the Senate and Democrats will hold onto their majority in the House of Representatives. Vilsack will garner 280 electoral votes or more.

2008 will prove to be a year of upsets for both Democrats and Republicans. The frontrunners will falter and new faces will pick up the batons and lead their Parties. Tom Vilsack will have the right stuff for the White House. Governors will continue to hold the edge in the Presidential sweepstakes. And, before you know it, the Presidential sweepstakes, version 2012, will be underway.

Bibliography

Felix, Antonia. *Wesley K. Clark: A Biography*. New York: Newmarket Press, 2004.

Clark, Wesley K. *Winning Modern Wars: Iraq, Terrorism and the American Empire*. New York: PublicAffairs, 2003.

Clinton, Hillary R. *Living History*. New York: Simon & Schuster, 2003.

Edwards, John. *Home: The Blueprints of Our Lives*. New York: Collins, 2006.

Gingrich, Newt. *Winning the Future: A 21st Century Contract with America*. Washington: Regnery Publishing, 2006.

Giuliani, Rudy. *Leadership*. New York: Miramax Books, 2005.

Gore, Al. *An Inconvenient Truth: The Planetary Emergency of Global Warming and What We Can Do About It*. New York: Rodale Books., 2006

Berens, Charlyne. *Chuck Hagel: Moving Forward*. Lincoln: University of Nebraska Press, 2006.

Huckabee, Mike. *From Hope to Higher Ground: 12 STOPS to Restoring America's Greatness*. New York: Center Street, 2007.

Butler, George. *John Kerry: A Portrait*. New York: Bulfinch, 2004.

McCain, John and Mark Salter. *Faith of My Fathers*. New York: Random House, 1999.

Obama, Barack. *The Audacity of Hope: Thoughts on Reclaiming the American Dream.* New York: Crown, 2006.

Pataki, George and Daniel Paisner. *Pataki: An Autobiography.* New York: Viking Adult, 1998.

Romney, Mitt. Turnaround: *Crisis, Leadership and the Olympic Games.* Washington: Regnery Publishing, 2004.

Index

978-0-595-42670-6

0-595-42670-0